Mutual Funds for Beginners

How to Invest in Mutual Funds for Safe Investing and Great Profits

by Charles E. Reinhardt

Table of Contents

Introduction

Mutual funds have become a popular investment tool for Americans saving for retirement or other financial goals. The act of investing in a mutual fund is simple — give the fund manager a call, or make the trade through your online brokerage account. The art lies in choosing the right fund. As the famous investor Benjamin Graham said, the returns depend *"...on the amount of intelligent effort the investor is willing and able to bring to bear on his task"* when choosing his investments. So, how can you benefit from professionally managed investments?

Here we will review whether a mutual fund is the right investment vehicle for you and how to make a sound investment to ensure great profits. You will become familiar with the tools you need to pick the right fund, and identify the factors that determine how long you should hold the investment. All you need is time for research and time to let your money grow.

Chapter 1: The Pros and Cons of Mutual Funds

To properly invest in a mutual fund, you need to understand how a mutual fund works and how it differs from other investments. What makes it the right investment vehicle for you?

A mutual fund is a professionally managed investment company whose shares are sold on the stock market. The fund is headed by a *money manager* who invests in a combination of stocks, bonds, money market funds, and other securities and assets. Mutual funds invest in hundreds to thousands of these securities to generate *capital gains* for investors. The fund's purchases are known as its *holdings* and make up the fund's *portfolio*.

To participate, you invest in the mutual fund with a minimum amount of money, and a money manager works with the fund that is pooled from many other investors like you. Every mutual fund has a *prospectus* that details the principles by which the money will be invested. The investors must trust that the money manager will adhere to these guidelines when investing the funds. These guidelines are quite strict—if the manager changes her strategy, she is likely to be accused of *style drift*.

Anyone can invest by buying shares of mutual funds. Investors can pull out of the investment at any time by selling their shares at the going price, and the investor's profit is the growth in share price since he invested multiplied by the number of shares he bought. Mutual funds are registered with the U.S. Security of Exchange and Commissions (SEC), meaning they have to conform to certain regulations. However, they are not insured by the Federal Deposit Insurance Corporation (FDIC), so there is no guarantee investors will not lose money investing in mutual funds.

It is important to understand the advantages and disadvantages of mutual funds relative to other investment instruments. This will guarantee that you are investing in the right vehicle that will bring the returns you expect.

Advantages

There are several reasons why mutual funds are a desirable investment. The two most cited advantages are the professional management and diversified assets. The fund manager is a highly qualified, experienced financial professional who is responsible for actively researching, choosing, and monitoring the underlying securities. This allows you as an investor with relatively small amounts of capital to have a stake in a sophisticated variety of investments, which would be difficult to otherwise do without lots of capital. Mutual funds generally perform better than bonds and index funds, because they have the know-how of an experienced manager guiding them.

This brings us to the diversified nature of the underlying securities. *Diversification* is the idea also known as not putting all your eggs in one basket. The fund manager selects securities from a wide range of companies, industries, and sectors. Therefore, even if one sector performs poorly, the losses from this sector are mitigated by the relatively strong performance of the other securities. It is important to recognize that holding several securities is not automatically equivalent to diversification; the manager must actively spread risk by choosing different types of investments.

Investors also enjoy high *liquidity* with mutual funds, which means one can buy and sell shares on any business day, as opposed to being committed to it for a certain amount of time which is the case with investing in bonds.

Disadvantages

The biggest downside to investing in mutual funds is that they charge a substantial amount of fees, which a lot of other investments nowadays do not do. These typically include a sales charge, annual fees, loads, and 12b-1 fees, which we will explain later. These can add up over time and eat into your returns, plus, the fees need to be paid even if the mutual fund does not perform well. There are minimum investment amounts, which can be difficult for shoestring investors. Unlike investing in individual stocks, the investor cedes control to the fund manager upon purchase of investment. Though investors have an idea of what the fund is comprised of, they are not privy to the exact securities and do not have any control over which securities are bought and sold. Finally, though the fund's total value is updated every day after the market closes, this is slow relative to the instantaneous update investors can get on stock information. For short-term investors and day traders, this can be difficult.

Chapter 2: The Different Types of Mutual Funds

Acquaint yourself with the types of mutual funds at the beginning of your research, as different types of funds suit different risk profiles. The main categories are money market funds, bond (or fixed-income) funds, and stock (or equity) funds.

Money market funds are comparatively low risk, as they are restricted by the SEC to only invest in high-quality, short-term investments. Rarely do their investors incur losses. But of course, low risk implies low return, and the returns for money-market funds are lower than bond or stock funds. There is also an "inflation risk," which occurs when inflation increases more than the investment returns and erodes the returns.

Bond funds are not restricted in their investments in the same way—they can invest in many different types of bonds. This means they are higher risk, but also likely to yield higher returns.

Stock funds are compiled of stocks, which generally perform better over time than corporate or government bonds and government-issued treasury securities. There are several types of stock funds. Growth funds include stocks that have potential for large capital gains: income funds pay regular dividends, index funds deliver the same returns as a particular market index by investing in all the companies of that index, and sector funds invest in securities from a particular industry, like technology.

Mutual funds are legally known as open-ended investment companies. Mutual funds can create and sell new shares continuously. Often, a mutual fund is confused with other similarly structured investments.

To avoid confusion, you also need to be aware of what a mutual fund is not. It is not a closed-ended fund, which sells a fixed number of shares in an initial public offering that later trade on a secondary market. And it is not a unit investment trusts (UIT), which makes a one-time public offering of a fixed number of securities that dissolve at a date specified during the creation of the UIT. It is not an exchange-traded fund (ETF) either, which trades shares on the secondary market and are generally bought and sold in bulk. ETFs aim to get the same return as a particular market index such as the NASDAQ or Dow Jones. Finally, do not make the common mistake of confusing mutual funds with hedge funds, which are private investment pools that are meant for an exclusive set of wealthy, sophisticated investors.

Chapter 3: Choosing the Right Fund Manager

The most important step in any investment decision is the research. It is the most time-consuming and resource-intensive, but also the most important step in ensuring great profits. After all, once you have chosen an investment, all you have left to do is invest the money and watch it pay you returns.

You may have heard of Vanguard and Fidelity Investments. Though these are popular mutual funds and may be good choices for your investment, it is advisable to look a little deeper before putting your money in any investment. After all, there are over 8,000 publicly traded mutual funds in the United States. How can you tell which is the best pick for you specifically?

The prospectus

The *prospectus* is the fund's selling document. The mutual fund is required to give you the prospectus *before* you invest. This document is updated yearly and contains the mutual fund's goals and strategies for investment. It will show you how the fund has been doing in the market historically along with forecasts for the future. The prospectus will also provide information about the fund managers and its advisers, the fees and other charges, and instructions on how to purchase shares. It also contains, by SEC mandate, the risks you assume by investing in the fund.

Evaluative reports

Fund reports by investment research firms such as Morningstar and the Mutual Fund Education Alliance will help you find the right mutual funds to fit your needs. You can refer to Morningstar's Analyst Picks for investing tips and expert analysis. However, there is a plethora of other online tools that can help you compare mutual funds. If you already use certain websites like MSN Money or Yahoo! Finance for other financial matters, use them to find information on mutual funds as well. Use a mutual fund cost calculator on the SEC website (sec.gov) to compare the costs of owning different funds *before* you buy.

Chapter 4: Setting Your Investment Goals

All this information can be daunting, but do not fear. We will take it step by step, starting from the top. Unsure where to start? Start with your own profile, and think about what you and your family need. With a pen and notebook, jot down your investment goals. The first things you need to identify are what you are saving for and when you need the money by. Then, we review below some metrics you can use to pick the right mutual fund to suit your risk profile and investment goals.

How in-depth you need to go roughly correlates to how long you will be holding the investment instrument before selling it. Casual investors, investing for years or decades in anticipation of college tuitions or retirement, will be well-prepared if they carefully understand the following details of the mutual fund:

- **Net asset value (NAV)**: To know what you need to invest in a mutual fund, you look for the net asset value. This is the total value of securities that the fund owns divided by the number of outstanding shares, or the number of shares held by investors. These values are updated every day after the market closes, as the price of the underlying securities and the number of outstanding shares change. If the fund holds stocks and bonds of $20 million and has 5 million outstanding shares, the NAV, and the price you pay excluding loads and fees, is $4. You can find the NAV by calling the fund's toll-free number, visiting its website, or looking on third-party financial websites

- **Long-term performance information**: How has the fund performed over the past 5, 10, or 20 years? The prospectus has valuable insight into performance in its risk/return bar chart and table, which shows you the fund's pre- and post-tax annual total returns over the last ten years. The same values are given for a composite benchmark index to provide you with some standard of comparison. However, to really understand the fund's objectives and performance, you need a point of comparison. Look online to compare the fund's performance with its "peer group", these are other funds which have similar objectives and strategies. It is a good sign if your pick performs well against both the benchmark index and members of its peer group.

- **Fees**: Since all mutual funds are registered with the SEC, they have to comply with the requirement to publish a fee table in their prospectus. This breaks down all the fees you may be subject to. Paying fees is not desirable as it eats into your returns, but these allow the mutual fund company, ultimately a profit-seeking business, to cover its costs. Fees are detailed below.

- **Expense ratios:** At the bottom of the prospectus' fee table will be the expense ratio, which sums all the fund's annual operating expenses as a fraction of its average net assets. This is useful to compare across funds. Once you have narrowed down your options, it is highly advisable to use a <u>mutual fund cost calculator</u> (you can find one on the SEC's official website) to compare your options.

- **Risk**: To assess the risk of investing in a particular mutual fund, keep your eye on two factors: the beta which measures the fund's volatility against the S&P 500, and the fund's biggest quarterly loss which shows you how bad things can get if you invest with them.

Mutual Fund Fees in Detail:

It is worthwhile to spend some more time on fees and expenses as they differentiate mutual funds from most other investments. They go towards paying the professional money manager who increases your returns, but they also eat away at those same returns over time.

A *load* is the cost of buying or selling shares of a mutual fund. It is the sales charge, and the most common fee in a mutual fund. Loaded mutual funds can sometimes charge 5% or more, and these fees go to the fund company and the broker. Generally, avoid loads. They are unnecessary losses. So why do they exist? Investment gurus might posit that loads lock you into a particular investment for a longer time— just like if you pay a $20 cover charge to get into a new bar you are likely to stay there longer than if you entered for free. This can be a win-win situation, because it keeps you invested beyond short-term fluctuations in the market, and the fund has more capital to work with. You are less likely to sell and pay another load for another investment. But paying a load is not in your best interest, and even avoiding loaded mutual funds will leave you with a whole lot of great options to choose from.

You have to be careful when reading the prospectus with regards to fees. Keep in mind that up until 0.25% per year, a fund can be labeled a *no-load fund*. Still, there may be other fees. For example, a *12b-1 fee* is something some mutual funds charge for their "distribution or service," essentially implying a fee to cover their marketing expenses. These fees should generally be avoided. Funds can charge several other fees, such as redemption fees (sales charge paid to the fund rather than the broker), account fees (charged for maintaining accounts, often when they are below a certain value), exchange fees, and purchase fees (similar to a load).

Understanding past performance, volatility, and risk:

A note about using past performance to estimate your returns: it is not a done deal. Past performance does not predict future performance, and this is because managers are constantly changing the underlying securities and the stock market is inherently unpredictable. When you can, and you should, use indicators of past performance to get an idea of how volatile the fund is. If this is too risky for your taste, look elsewhere. How do you know how much risk you can take? Remember that volatility is smoothed over time with the general upward trend of the market, so short-term investments are riskier. For example, if you are investing your retirement money, you might be fine with volatile investments since you are investing for the long-term. However, if there is a chance that you could need that money sooner, and you may use it as an emergency fund five years from now, you will find risk less acceptable than someone investing it for 20 years. Risk not only depends on your financial goals but also your personal preference. If you know you would rather not see your returns swing up and down, even if it results in high returns, stick with low-risk (and low-return) investments.

Remember, the money market is less risky than bonds, which in turn is less risky than stocks. So if you are saving for the short term, look to money market funds. Investing long term? You can feel comfortable with the volatility of stocks. Somewhere in the middle? Bonds are good for financial goals that are five to ten years into the future, and you can balance your portfolio with money market and stock investments.

Tax Consequences:

With mutual funds, you must pay an income tax on any dividends you receive from the fund in a particular year. When you sell your shares, your personal capital gains will be taxed. In addition, as a member of the mutual fund you will be also be taxed on the fund's capital gains. If a fund collects income through dividends or by selling securities for a profit, shareholders have to chip in to pay those taxes. This means you may be paying taxes even though you didn't personally collect capital gains from the fund. Steer clear of big tax hits by investing in tax-efficient funds and tax-exempt funds.

Chapter 5: Managing Your Investment

Once you have decided on a mutual fund, pause and congratulate yourself! Making the transaction is relatively simple compared to all the pre-purchase research. You can buy directly from the mutual fund, although people generally go through banks or brokers, either by making a phone call or doing it online. In addition to the current NAV per share, keep in mind that you will be charged any front-end load and other fees as detailed in the prospectus. Note that you do not purchase mutual funds from a secondary market such as the New York Stock Exchange or the NASDAQ Stock Market.

Tracking

What is there to do next after purchasing shares? Investing is a funny thing. It requires patience, leaving your investments alone to let them grow beyond short-term market fluctuations. But it also requires careful monitoring because you have to know if it is performing as expected. After all, even if your fund had performed well in the past, there is no guarantee that it will continue to perform well. You must track its performance. You can do this online, or by the monthly or quarterly shareholder statement you are required to receive from the mutual fund firm. It is important to safely store these statements, for accounting purposes as well as tracking. Track all the metrics that you used to make your selection, and make sure they do not stray far from your expectations.

Divesting

Successful mutual fund investors always know from the onset how long they want to keep their money in a certain fund. Generally, financial experts do not suggest pulling out investments when the market is not doing so well. In the case of mutual funds, there are some circumstances under which you might consider divesting sooner than you originally intended.

- Based on a regular overview of the quarterly statements, you may find that the portfolio has been rebalanced in a way that increases risk or that moves away from achieving the objectives stated in the prospectus. This is known as "style drift." This can be dangerous and should cause you to consider transferring the investment.

- Another common reason for divesting from a mutual fund is a change in managers. Often managers are careful to stick to a certain recognizable style, but as can happen with change in leadership, a new manager can rock the boat in ways that the shareholders do not appreciate.

- The expense ratio may rise, making it too large to be worth your while.

Remember that these performance-related issues will be reflected in the prospectus and online data—your mutual fund will decrease in rank relative to the benchmark, or the listed expense ratio will rise relative to its peer groups.

There are personal reasons to divest as well. You may be moving closer to retirement and want to shift to financial investments with generally higher returns, like stocks. You may have grown more comfortable with researching about financial opportunities and have found something better! These are all possible and valid reasons to pull out of your investment. However, always consider the pros and cons of divesting very carefully before making a decision.

You pull out of a mutual fund quite like how you pull out of a stock: make a phone call to whoever executed the trade for you, or if you have online access, sell your shares. Selling shares is akin to taking your money out of their fund. You will have to specify how you want to receive your profits, either as a check, bank transfer, or as credit in your brokerage account so you may reinvest it, usually without paying another sales load.

Conclusion

Successfully investing in a mutual fund is not rocket science. It only requires diligence and realistic financial goals. Most of your efforts will go into research, so take your time and compare the performance and fee tables of as many different funds as you can. By the time you have chosen a mutual fund you should be able to explain your investment decision in layman's terms and provide a basic idea of the fund's details. From then on, if you stay aware of fee hikes and tax risks and if you watchfully track your fund's performance, you will likely reap great profits from your sound investment. Happy investing!

Finally, I'd like to thank you for purchasing this book! If you enjoyed it or found it helpful, I'd greatly appreciate it if you'd take a moment to leave a review on Amazon. Thank you!

Made in the USA
Coppell, TX
19 March 2020